SUPER
SANDCASTLE·
Going Green

WHAT
IN THE
WORLD
IS A
GREEN SCHOOL?

Oona Gaarder-Juntti

Consulting Editor, Diane Craig, M.A./Reading Specialist

ABDO
Publishing Company

Published by ABDO Publishing Company, 8000 West 78th Street, Edina, Minnesota 55439. Copyright © 2011 by Abdo Consulting Group, Inc. International copyrights reserved in all countries. No part of this book may be reproduced in any form without written permission from the publisher. Super SandCastle™ is a trademark and logo of ABDO Publishing Company.

Printed in the United States of America, North Mankato, Minnesota
052010
092010

 PRINTED ON RECYCLED PAPER

Editor: Katherine Hengel
Content Developer: Nancy Tuminelly
Cover and Interior Design and Production: Oona Gaarder-Juntti, Mighty Media
Photo Credits: AbleStock, Shutterstock

Library of Congress Cataloging-in-Publication Data

Gaarder-Juntti, Oona, 1979-
  What in the world is a green school? / Oona Gaarder-Juntti.
    p. cm. -- (Going green)
  ISBN 978-1-61613-190-6
  1. School buildings--Environmental aspects--Juvenile literature. I. Title.
  LB3241.2.G33 2011
  371.6--dc22
                            2010004324

Super SandCastle™ books are created by a team of professional educators, reading specialists, and content developers around five essential components— phonemic awareness, phonics, vocabulary, text comprehension, and fluency— to assist young readers as they develop reading skills and strategies and increase their general knowledge. All books are written, reviewed, and leveled for guided reading, early reading intervention, and Accelerated Reader® programs for use in shared, guided, and independent reading and writing activities to support a balanced approach to literacy instruction.

ABOUT SUPER SANDCASTLE™

Bigger Books for Emerging Readers

Grades K–4

Created for library, classroom, and at-home use, Super SandCastle™ books support and engage young readers as they develop and build literacy skills and will increase their general knowledge about the world around them. Super SandCastle™ books are an extension of SandCastle™, the leading preK–3 imprint for emerging and beginning readers. Super SandCastle™ features a larger trim size for more reading fun.

Let Us Know

Super SandCastle™ would like to hear your stories about reading this book. What was your favorite page? Was there something hard that you needed help with? Share the ups and downs of learning to read. We want to hear from you! Send us an e-mail.

sandcastle@abdopublishing.com

Contact us for a complete list of SandCastle™, Super SandCastle™, and other nonfiction and fiction titles from ABDO Publishing Company.

www.abdopublishing.com • 8000 West 78th Street
Edina, MN 55439 • 800-800-1312 • 952-831-1632 fax

Contents

WHAT IN THE WORLD IS BEING GREEN?

Being green means taking care of the earth. Many things on our planet are connected. When one thing changes, it can cause something else to change. That's why the way we treat the earth is so important. Keeping the earth healthy can seem like a big job. You can help by saving energy and **resources** every day.

Saving Energy

Schools need energy for things such as buses and heat. This energy often comes from burning oil and coal. This creates greenhouse gases. These gases go into the air. They can trap the sun's heat and make the earth warmer. This is called **global** warming. Saving energy reduces greenhouse gases.

Protecting Resources

Soil, trees, water, and air are natural **resources**. Sometimes we waste or harm the earth's resources. For example, throwing paper in the trash wastes resources. It can be recycled!

GREEN SCHOOLS

Schools are big buildings. They use a lot of energy and **resources**. That's why it's important for schools to go green! Some schools get energy from **solar panels**. Others have their own vegetable gardens!

Talk with your principal. Does your school recycle paper? What about food scraps? There are many things you can do. Let's learn more about green schools!

Did you know?

Plastic bottles can last up to 450 years in a **landfill**.

Did you know?

One school bus can carry about 60 kids. It would take at least 15 cars to do that!

Did you know?

Recycled paper is used to make paper towels, notebooks, envelopes, and boxes.

IN A GREEN WORLD

The things we do at school can affect the earth. Here are some simple ways to go green in your classroom!

Write on both sides of each piece of paper. Recycle paper instead of throwing it in the trash.

REDUCE REUSE RECYCLE

Use up your school supplies before you buy new ones. Buy notebooks made from recycled paper.

IN A GREEN WORLD

A lot of things get thrown away at lunchtime.
How can you make less garbage?

Use a lunch box
instead of paper bags.

Plastic **containers** are better than
plastic bags. You can wash and
reuse them.

Take the school bus or share a ride with a friend. This is a good way to reduce air **pollution** and save gas.

Ride your bike or scooter to school with your friends.

13

HOW YOU CAN HELP

Everyone knows the 3 Rs. Reduce, Reuse, and Recycle. Do you know how to practice the 3 Rs at school? The next few pages will show you how! Think about how you get to school every day. What **resources** do you use when you're there? There are many simple ways to be green at school!

Energy Detective

Want to save energy at your school? Become an energy detective! Learn about the **resources** your school uses. How can you cut back and save energy?
Start with these questions.

- What kind of energy heats and cools your school in the winter?

- What kind of energy does your school bus run on?

- What kind of energy runs your lights and computers?

- What kind of things does your school recycle?

- What things can we do to save more energy?

Zero Waste

All those juice boxes, plates, and sandwich bags add up! Try to pack a no-waste lunch.

Start with a lunch box. Pack your food in **containers** that you can use again. Bring a reusable water bottle and a cloth napkin if you can. If you eat all your food, that cuts down on waste too.

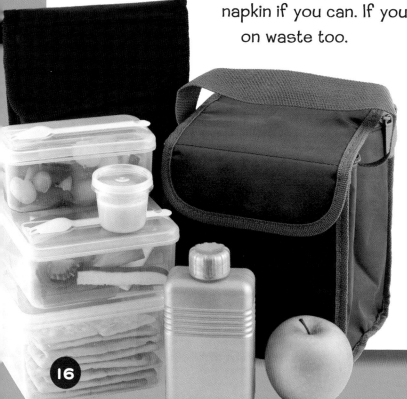

About 2.5 million plastic bottles are thrown away every hour in the United States.

Paper Challenge

Are there recycling bins at your school? If not, talk to your teacher about getting some. Remember to use both sides of a piece of paper before it's recycled.

Get the whole school involved! Start a contest to see which class can recycle the most paper.

GO GREEN. USE LESS PAPER.

Recycling 1 ton (907 kg) of paper saves 17 trees. The average school uses 38 tons (34,473 kg) of paper each year.

Green Transportation

Do you live close to your school? Ask your parents if you can walk, bike, or skate to school. Maybe you can go with a friend who lives near you. Or take the bus or share a ride. When a group of friends ride together, it's called carpooling.

Maybe you could take a walking bus to school! Find some kids who can walk to school with you. Have an adult be the "bus" driver. Then "pick up" your friends along the way!

Energy Team

Start a student energy patrol! Make sure the lights are off in empty classrooms. Remind people to use natural light whenever it is available.

Make sure the computers at your school are in energy-saving **mode**. Also, make sure the monitors are off when the computers are not in use.

Get the whole school involved! Ask if you can put up posters about saving energy.

Learn More

Ask your teacher if you can learn more about the **environment** and ways to protect it. You can also research different environmental groups on your own. Find one that you'd like to support. Then have a bake sale to raise money! Make sure to get permission first. This is a great way to care for the earth.

Save Our Oceans

Litter-Free Zone

Make sure your garbage goes into a trash can. If you can't find a trash can, hold onto it. You can throw it away later.

Picking up trash is very rewarding. You can see a big difference in a short time. All you need are some gloves and a garbage bag!

TRASH ONLY

PLEASE RECYCLE

Ask your teacher if your class can adopt an area around your school. Your class will keep the area litter free. You might **inspire** other students too!

LET'S THINK GREEN

There is a lot to learn about being green at school! Remember that small things count. That is why it is important to build green habits now! What other things can you do to make a difference?

Taking care of the earth is everyone's responsibility. That means kids and adults! Talk with your teachers and friends about being green at school. Let's all work hard together and think green!

TAKE THE GREEN PLEDGE

I promise to help the earth every day by doing things in a different way.

At school I can help by:

♻ Packing a waste-free lunch.

♻ Recycling paper and using both sides.

♻ Taking the bus, carpooling, or walking to school.

♻ Turning off lights and computers in an empty classroom.

GLOSSARY

aluminum – a light metal often used to make cans and bottles.

container – something that other things can be put into.

environment – nature and everything in it, such as the land, sea, and air.

global – having to do with the whole earth.

inspire – to fill someone with emotion.

landfill – a place where garbage is stacked and then covered up with earth.

mode – a way to do something.

pollution – contamination of the air, water, or soil caused by man-made waste.

resource – the supply or source of something. A *natural resource* is a resource found in nature, such as water or trees.

solar panel – a device that turns the sun's light into energy.